RANDOM ACTS OF KINDNESS

An Illustrated Celebration

METRO BOOKS
NEW YORK

This 2010 edition published by Metro Books.

Portions of this text appeared in slightly different
form in *Random Acts of Kindness* (2002), *More Random
Acts of Kindness* (2007), and *Practice Random Acts of
Kindness* (2007).

Cover and text design by Tracy Johnson
Cover and text illustration © ShadyMaple/
iStockphoto.com

Metro Books
122 Fifth Avenue
New York, NY 10011

ISBN: 978-1-4351-2551-3

Printed and bound in Hong Kong

10 9 8 7 6 5 4 3 2 1

When you carry out acts of kindness
you get a wonderful feeling inside.
It is as though something inside your
body responds and says,
"yes, this is how I ought to feel."

—RABBI HAROLD KUSHNER

INTRODUCTION

So many gods, so many creeds,
So many paths that wind and wind,
While just the art of being kind
Is all the sad world needs.

—Ella Wheeler Wilcox

Our world can seem like a sad place. Open the newspaper
and draw in the suffering, the pain, the palpable sense of lack.
Or, occasionally, read something that lifts the spirits, like a
Thanksgiving Day article about a mother who must choose
between making her mortgage payment and sending money
to her daughter for groceries. She misdials her daughter's
phone number, and the stranger who gets the recorded
message gets in touch with the family and delivers enough
groceries for a turkey feast and to feed them until the next
paycheck comes. "I helped people," says the Good Samaritan.
"I think it's what anybody would have done."

The stories in this book are as varied as the people telling them, but at the foundation of each is a very simple and compassionate connection between strangers who, for a moment, experienced one another not as strangers, but as family. In a sense, kindness truly *is* the acting out of our deep and real connection to everyone and everything around us. It is the realization that all of us are in fact—not just in theory or theology—in this together.

Kindness is what we do, person to person, moment to moment. It is about being who we truly are. Its power is not only easily accessible to anyone who cares to use it, but it also can never be diminished; it expands with every action. It has the ability to utterly transform another person's life through the simplest of actions. It has the capacity to return us to the very core of our humanity. Kindness can and does open hearts, erase boundaries, and change lives. Here's to celebrating the glorious acts of kindness commemorated in these pages, to the many more happening all over the world right this moment, and to the many yet to come!

The quality of mercy is not strained,
it dropeth as the gentle rain from heaven
upon the place beneath. It is twice blessed:
it blesseth him that giveth and him that takes.

—*William Shakespeare*

Kindness is twice blessed. It blesses the one who gives it with a sense of his or her own capacity to love, and the person who receives it with a sense of the beneficence of the universe. Kindness heals us, because it reminds us of our oneness, allows us to see ourselves in one another's eyes, to remember that eyes themselves are a miracle, that seeing is a gift, and that the other person, no matter who he or she may be, is, in one way or another, a perfect reflection of ourselves.

The power of kindness is immense. It is nothing less, really, than the power to change the world.

—DAPHNE ROSE KINGMA

When I was quite small my immigrant Russian grandmother told me that people in this country give from the wrong place. "When you give from here," she declared, pointing to her solar plexus, "it's like keeping a ledger book. That's not giving, that's trading. I give you three so you give me three. I sweep the floor so you carry the bundles."

She pushed the wisps of white hair out of her eyes with the backs of her red hands, shaking her head back and forth, tsk-ing her tongue against her teeth. "You give your soul away when you give like that. Giving is supposed to be from here," she said, pointing to the center of her chest with a feathery finger. "When you give from your heart, it's not so you get anything back. There is no owing or owed. You just give because you want to give. When you give like this, it fills you up. Your heart can never run out. The more you give from there, the fuller you will be . . . When you give like this, there are no strangers."

—DAWNA MARKOVA

SEVERAL YEARS AGO, when I was living in Chicago, I read in the newspaper about a little boy who had leukemia. Every time he was feeling discouraged or particularly sick, a package would arrive for him containing some little toy or book to cheer him up with a note saying the present was from the Magic Dragon. No one knew who it was. Eventually the boy died and his parents thought the Magic Dragon would finally come forth and reveal him or herself. But that never happened. After hearing the story, I resolved to become a Magic Dragon whenever I could, and have had many occasions.

If there is any kindness I can show,
or any good thing I can do to any fellow being,
let me do it now, and not deter or neglect it,
as I shall not pass this way again.

—William Penn

Who would ever think that a telephone answering machine could change your life? I had just broken up from a long and very painful relationship and found myself suddenly in a new city without friends, without anything to do or any desire to do anything. I was like a listless blob of expended energy. Every day I would come home from work and just stare at the walls, sometimes crying but mostly just sitting and wondering if this cloud would ever go away.

I had bought an answering machine—why, I don't know, since nobody ever called me. One night I came home and the red light was flashing. I couldn't believe it—a phone call. When I played it back, a wonderful male voice started to apologize that he had called the wrong number, and I burst into tears. But then he kept talking. He said my voice on the message had sounded so sad and he just wanted to tell me that it was okay to be sad, that being able to feel that sadness was important. His message went on for almost twenty minutes, just talking about how important it was to be able to go through the pain instead of running away from it, and how even though it probably seemed impossible now, things would get better. He never even said his name, but that message was, in a very important way, the beginning of my life.

We do not remember days, we remember moments.

—Cesare Pavese

The purpose of life
is a life of purpose.
—ROBERT BYRNE

**Do every act of your life
as if it were your last.**

–Marcus Aurelius

This is the true joy of life, the being used up for a purpose recognized by yourself as a mighty one; being a force of nature instead of a feverish, selfish little clod of ailments and grievances, complaining that the world will not devote itself to making you happy. I am of the opinion that my life belongs to the community, and as long as I live, it is my privilege to do for it whatever I can. I want to be thoroughly used up when I die, for the harder I work, the more I live. Life is no "brief candle" to me. It is a sort of splendid torch which I have got hold of for a moment, and I want to make it burn as brightly as possible before handing it on to future generations.

—George Bernard Shaw

TWO DAYS BEFORE MY FIFTIETH BIRTHDAY I had a heart attack. It was a most surprising random act of kindness. I had lived the previous thirty years of my life as a powerful, successful, and amazingly productive man. I had also lived so cut off from my emotions that I couldn't even fathom what the whole fuss about feelings was all about. I had worn out the efforts of three good women, took pride in my unfeeling logic, denied that there was anything wrong or missing in my life, and was prepared to march stubbornly forward.

Until I was felled and terrified by my own heart. That experience unlocked a lifetime of buried emotions. So, without knowing it, when the doctors revived me, they delivered me to a life fuller and more beautiful than I had ever imagined.

If you bring forth what is inside of you,
what you bring forth will save you.
If you don't bring forth what is inside of you,
**what you don't bring forth
will destroy you.**

—Jesus

We cannot live only for ourselves. A thousand fibers connect us with our fellow men; and among those fibers, as sympathetic threads, our actions run as causes, and they come back to us as effects.

—HERMAN MELVILLE

I am done with great things and big plans, great institutions and big success. I am for those tiny, invisible loving human forces that work from individual to individual, creeping through the crannies of the world like so many rootlets, or like the capillary oozing of water, which, if given time, will rent the hardest monuments of pride.

—*William James*

FEAR grows out of the things we think;
it lives in our minds.
COMPASSION grows out of the things we are,
and lives in our hearts.

—Barbara Garrison

WE HAD JUST SEARCHED A SMALL VILLAGE that had been suspected of harboring Vietcong. We really tore the place up—it wasn't hard to do—but had found nothing. Just up the trail from the village we were ambushed. I got hit and don't remember anything more until I woke up with a very old Vietnamese woman leaning over me. Before I passed out again I remembered seeing her in the village we had just destroyed and I knew I was going to die. When I woke again, the hole in my left side had been cleaned and bandaged, and the woman was leaning over me again offering me a cup of warm tea. As I was drinking the tea and wondering why I was still alive, a helicopter landed nearby to take me back. The woman quietly got up and disappeared down the trail.

Some day, after we have mastered
the winds, the waves, the tides, and gravity,
we shall harness the energies of love.
Then, for the second time in the history of
the world, man will have discovered fire.

—PIERRE TEILHARD DE CHARDIN

I live high in the hills and my body is getting old. One day I was out in my garden fussing with weeds and grew tired. I decided to lie back on the grass and rest like I used to when I was a small boy. I woke up some minutes later with a neighbor whom I had never met leaning over me, all out of breath, asking me if I was okay. He had looked out his window two blocks up the hill and seen me lying on my back on the grass, looking, I am sure, like the victim of a stroke or heart attack, and had run all the way down the hill to check on me. It was embarrassing, but it was also so wonderfully touching. After we had sorted it all out, he let out a deep breath and lay down on the grass beside me. We both stayed there very quietly for a while and then he said, "thank you for deciding to take your nap out on the lawn where I could see you. The sky is such a beautiful thing and I cannot remember the last time I really looked at it."

It is one of the most beautiful compensations of life that no man can sincerely try to help another without helping himself.

—Ralph Waldo Emerson

This only is charity,
to do all, all that we can.

—John Donne

I was living in Chicago and going through what was a particularly cold winter—both in temperature and in my personal life. One evening I was walking home from a bar where I had been drinking alone, feeling sorry for myself, when I saw a homeless man standing over an exhaust grate in front of a department store. He was wearing a filthy sportcoat and approaching everyone who passed by for money.

I was too immersed in my own troubles to deal with him so I crossed the street. As I went by, I looked over and saw a businessman come out of the store and pull a ski parka out of a bag and hand it to the homeless man. For a moment both the man and I were frozen in time as the businessman turned and walked away. Then the man looked across the street at me. He shook his head slowly and I knew he was crying. It was the last time I have ever been able to disappear into my own sorrow.

When I was going through a very difficult time,
someone called me up and played piano music for me
on my answering machine. It made me feel very loved—
and I never discovered who had done it.

**Give light, and the
darkness will disappear
of itself.**

—Erasmus

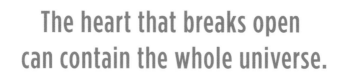

The heart that breaks open
can contain the whole universe.

—*Joanna Macy*

**Experience praises the most happy
the one who made the most people happy.**

—KARL MARX

The beginning and end of Torah
is performing acts of loving kindness.

—*The Talmud*

I AM A CORPORATE LAWYER, and several years ago I was at my first closing. The investment banker came to deliver a check for $55 million to my client, and before my client arrived, I went to the Xerox machine to copy the check for our records. I put the check in the feeder of the copier, and it promptly shredded it! I told the banker about the mutilated check, and a moment later my client arrived, eager to receive the money. The banker looked at me and said to the client, "I can't believe it! I forgot the check!" He left and returned an hour later with a new check, and I kept my job.

My husband and I travel a lot, and at the time this happened I had a horse, a wonderful horse. We were out of town when a one-hundred-mile endurance horse race (that's a race where people from all over New England get together and travel as fast as they can for one hundred miles) went right past our driveway. My horse, whose name was Dusty, decided that she wanted to join the race. So she jumped over the fence. Galloped off. No saddle. Nobody on her back.

The next day when my husband and I returned home there was a note on the door from the sheriff saying that my horse had gone back to the barn on the other side of town where she had been born eighteen years before. So I drove there. It was a lovely old farm, owned by people I didn't know.

The new owners were a man, his wife, and their children, two little girls ages seven and five. And sure enough, there in the corral behind the barn were the two girls and Dusty. The man told me that that morning when they had gotten up, the little girls had started screaming because at the top of the hill, with the sun rising behind her, was this beautiful palomino horse. They lured her into their corral and proceeded to spend the day brushing her and treating her a lot better than she had been for many years under my sometimes care.

They looked so happy. The seven-year-old girl turned and, with a trembling lip, said, "Can I ride her before you take her back?" I said that she could have her for another half-hour or so. And then I went to the local general store and bought a bottle of apple cider. When I returned, the girls told me that they had always wished for a horse but their parents really didn't have the money for one. I sat them down and told them I was going to give them Dusty. And that I wanted them to promise me that someday when they were grown up they each would find a little girl—a little girl they didn't know—and give her some very special gift that she had always wanted.

Then we celebrated with a bubbling glass of apple cider, toasting to Dusty.

It is in the shelter of each other that the people live.

—IRISH PROVERB

FOR YEARS, the Oakland, California neighbors watched as Mary's house and yard slowly decayed. Mary was an elderly, wheelchair-bound widow who could no longer manage the necessary repairs and maintenance on her house. One day a couple of neighbors—a bus driver and an auto worker—went down to the city's Office of Community Development, got forty-five gallons of Mary's favorite color of paint and a handful of painting supplies, and set to work. By the time they had finished, they had also put in a new lawn, cut back the tangled shrubs, and topped off the paint job with eye-catching trim.

Our deeds determine us,
just as much as we determine our deeds.

—GEORGE ELIOT

Whenever you are to do a thing, though it can never be known but to yourself, ask yourself how you would act were all the world looking at you and act accordingly.

—Thomas Jefferson

Do everything with a mind that lets go.
Do not expect praise or reward.

-Achaan Chah

My grandmother was born in Russia at a time of great confusion and instability. She immigrated to this country as a young girl and ended up marrying a man who was extraordinarily successful. She could have lived in the fanciest neighborhood and eaten only at the best restaurants; instead she lived in a very modest area and would go to Woolworth's for coffee. In those days, a cup of coffee cost five cents, and whenever my grandmother would buy a cup, she would always leave a five-dollar tip. Her explanation was simple: "They work hard for their money."

Man should not consider his
material possessions his own,
but common to all,
so as to share them without
hesitation when others are in need.

—ST. THOMAS AQUINAS

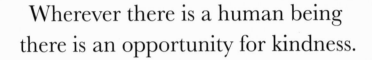

Wherever there is a human being
there is an opportunity for kindness.

—Seneca

AN ACT OF KINDNESS can sometimes take incredible courage. I was at the county fair with my mother many years ago. I remember it was a very, very hot day and all around us children and parents were melting down. We were walking behind a woman with two small children. The children were crying and whining and the mother was getting increasingly upset. Finally she started to scream at them to shut up; then she turned around and stuck them both very hard. Just to see this happen right in front of me made me feel like I had been hit as well.

Of course her kids started crying even more and the mother was on the verge of completely losing control when my mother walked up to her, touched her arm, and said something like, "You poor dear, don't worry, sometimes things just get out of control for a moment." Then my mother offered to take the children over to the ice cream stand, buy them some ice cream, and sit with them while the woman took a little walk to compose herself. She returned about ten minutes later, thanked my mother, hugged her children, and went on.

When I was in college, I worked part-time at a sporting goods store. There was a kid who would come by two or three times a week to visit with this baseball mitt that he wanted to buy. My manager and I would joke about him not only because he was so dedicated and persistent, but also because he had picked the best and most expensive mitt in the store to obsess over.

This went on for months. The kid would come in, and you could tell he was so relieved that the mitt was still there. He would put it on, pound his fist into the pocket a couple of times, and then very carefully put it back onto the shelf and leave. Finally, one day he came in with a shoebox and a smile about eight miles wide and announced that he wanted to buy the mitt. So the manager brought the mitt over to the cash register while the kid counted out a shoebox worth of nickels, quarters, and dimes. His stash came to exactly $19.98. The mitt cost $79.98, not including tax. My manager looked at the price tag, and sure enough the number 7 was a little smudged, enough that a desperately hopeful seven-year-old could imagine it to be a 1. Then he looked at me, smiled, and very carefully recounted. "Yep, exactly $19.98." Wrapping up the mitt, he gave it to the boy.

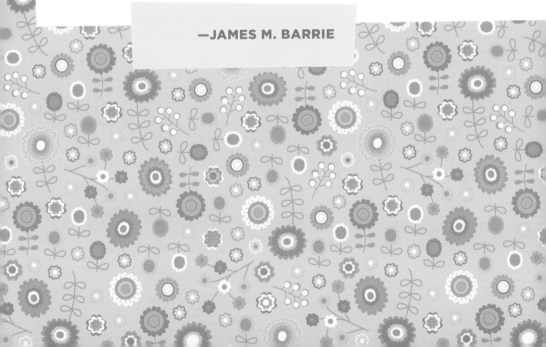

Shall we make a new rule of life
from tonight: always to try to be
a little kinder than is necessary.

—JAMES M. BARRIE

You hear stories about tourists trying to drive in San Francisco all the time. I discovered a whole new twist one day when I was walking up a particularly steep hill and saw a car stopped near the top with a very frightened woman inside. As I watched, she made a few attempts to get moving but each time seemed to lose more ground than she gained. Then a man came out of the corner market. The next thing I know, she gets out of the car and goes around to the passenger side while he climbs into the driver's seat and promptly drives the car up over the top of the dreaded hill. By then, I had reached the store where the helpful man's wife was standing, watching the proceedings. She told me that her husband, who owns the market, has been doing that for years, and that during the summertime—peak tourist season—he will "rescue" as many as ten scared drivers a week.

The only justification for
ever looking down on somebody
is to pick them up.

—Jesse Jackson

WHEN I WAS IN HIGH SCHOOL, I had a friend who asked me to help him plant some weeping willow trees down by a creek. It seems that he had watched every year as the banks of this creek had been increasingly eaten away. It had gotten to the point where the water was threatening to overflow into the nearby housing development. My friend had obviously done his research; he found out that willows grew quickly, easily, and with a great spreading root system that drinks up lots of water and would stabilize the creek bank. When I met him at the creek, he had a huge bundle of willow branches in his arms. We spent most of the day planting these willow sprigs up and down the endangered curve.

Many years later, I was home visiting and found myself walking down by that creek. Where we spent that afternoon is now a beautiful idyllic bend with a long curving row of large graceful willows bending out over the water.

It is the mark of a good action
that it appears inevitable in retrospect.

—ANONYMOUS

I had just graduated from college and had gone back to the town I grew up in to visit friends. My parents had sold the family home a few years back and moved out of state, so I also took the opportunity to drive by the old house just to see it. Out in the front yard, perched in "my" giant oak tree, was a boy about ten years old. I stopped the car, went over to introduce myself, and told the boy that when I was his age I practically lived in that tree. He thought that was real funny because he said his mother was always telling people that he lives in that tree.

While we were standing there talking, laughing, and feeling very good about our shared tree, a car drove up to the curb right in front of us. A middle-aged man got out of the driver's side, came around to the passenger side, and helped a very frail-looking old man out of the car. I guess we were both staring, but the old man just walked right up to the tree, patted it on the side, looked at us, and said, "I planted this tree sixty years ago when there was nothing here but fields. I still like to come visit it now and then." Then he turned around, got back into the car, and drove away. We were both so shocked we didn't say a word until after the old man had left. Then the boy just looked at me and said, "Wow."

Blessed is the influence of
one true, loving, human soul on another.

—*George Eliot*

If you are unfaithfully here, you are causing great damage.
But if your love is joined to the great Love,
you are helping people you don't know and have never met.

—RUMI

One kind word can warm three winter months.

—JAPANESE PROVERB

Complete possession is proved only by giving.
All you are unable to give possesses you.

—ANDRÉ GIDE

$\mathcal{M}$y religion is very simple. My religion is kindness.

—*The Dalai Lama*

Everything that is not given is lost.

—Indian proverb

There was a time in my life when everything was working so smoothly, I found myself sitting at home one Saturday with all my work done and household chores completed and that delicious feeling of having nothing to do. Then I thought about a friend from work who was a single mother of two small children and never seemed to have the time for anything. I jumped into my car, drove over to her house, walked in, and said, "Put me to work." At first she didn't really believe it, but we ended up having a great time, cleaning like mad, taking time out to feed and play with the kids, and then diving back into the chores.

For many years, our next-door neighbor was this very sweet and unusual old woman. Her husband had died quite young and she had lived alone ever since her children grew up and moved out. When my brother and I were young, she always treated us as real people, not just a couple of kids. She would talk to us seriously about what was happening in our lives, and actually took an interest in things like the wins and losses of our baseball teams. She also had what at the time was a really hot car—a silver 1957 Chevy—that she took great care of. As she got older, her son took over the duties of occasionally washing and polishing the car, but then he moved out of state.

One day my brother and I were at our parents' house for Thanksgiving dinner and we noticed that the neighbor's poor old Chevy was looking very sad. Later that night we snuck into her driveway, washed the car inside and out, waxed it, and polished all the chrome; when we were done it was shining just like a floor model.

That was nearly five years ago, and since then we have made regular guerrilla raids into her driveway. I don't think she knows who is doing it, but my mother reports that she has taken to going "cruising" in her car, and always laughs and tells my mother she has an "automotive angel."

SEVERAL MONTHS AGO, I found myself driving in Los Angeles through morning rush hour traffic. Traffic was heavy, but everyone was going quite fast. Suddenly a white Mazda RX7 in the slow lane spun out, doing four complete circles across the freeway. I stared in disbelief as cars swerved to avoid the whirling white dervish. By some miracle, all the traffic missed the car, which came to rest on the opposite side of the freeway, in the fast lane, facing the wrong way. No one stopped; everyone continued as though nothing had happened.

I pulled off the freeway, got out of my car, walked to the Mazda, opened the door, and pulled out a sobbing, hysterical woman who kept saying, "Did you see what they did? They ran me off the road." I put my arms around the woman, who collapsed into them and sobbed as though her heart would break. She finally calmed down enough to explain that a blue Bronco had forced her off the road, causing her car to spin out. There we stood—two women, total strangers, holding and comforting

A friend who was working in the Dominican Republic with Habitat for Humanity had befriended a small boy named Etin. He noticed that when Etin wore a shirt it was always the same dirty, tattered one. A box of used clothes had been left at the camp, and my friend found two shirts in it that were in reasonably good shape and about Etin's size, so he gave them to the grateful boy. A few days later he saw another boy wearing one of the shirts. When he next met up with Etin he explained that the shirts were meant for him. Etin just looked at him and said, "But you gave me two!"

DRIVING THE FOURTEEN MILES HOME to our small Iowa town from a last-minute Christmas shopping trip, my father was carefully navigating his way through the heavy falling snow. About a half-mile from our farmhouse—the only one for miles—we spotted a car in the ditch and stopped to investigate. It was empty. The blowing snow all but obscured the lane up to our house, but I could see that the lights were on and we *never* left the lights on.

As we stumbled in our front door we were greeted by the refugees from the abandoned car, a stranded family of four. They began apologizing for being in our house, but Mom just said, "Shush, you did what you had to do," as she began preparing hot drinks and food for us all.

It seemed so natural to expect them to stay the night, so my brother and I eagerly began getting acquainted with our new friends. Farm life was lonely for the two of us, ages eight and ten, and the company of other boys was always welcome. That night the full force of the storm hit and by morning it was obvious that our guests would not be able to continue on their journey to Minnesota for Christmas. There was two feet of snow everywhere and probably no snowplow for days. To four small boys it was paradise.

Mom took us aside and we began to rewrap and address presents for our newfound extended family. Unbeknownst to us, the father had gone back to their car to collect their Minnesota presents and was doing the same. It was one of the best Christmases I can remember.

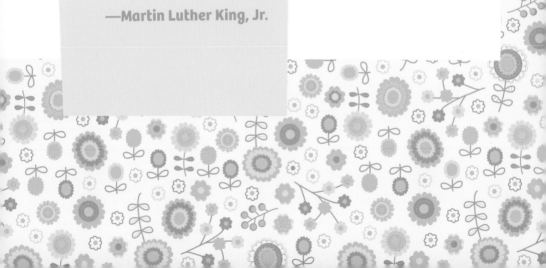

Life's most persistent and urgent question is,
What are you doing for others?

—Martin Luther King, Jr.

Even as a mother protects with her life
Her child, her only child,
So with a boundless heart
Should one cherish all living beings;
Radiating kindness over the entire world.

—Buddha

Let us be kinder to one another.

—Aldous Huxley, on his deathbed

An adventurous group of Australians had arrived in Nepal for an attempt to climb Mount Everest. At the ten-thousand-foot level, one in the group became very sick with chills, fever, nausea, and vomiting. His "friends" wrapped him up in his sleeping bag and continued their climb. Two weeks later, he woke up in a Sherpa village. The Sherpas had found him on the mountainside, where he had slipped into a coma, and had brought him to their village to nurse him back to health.

It took many months for him to fully regain his health. Finally, six months after being abandoned on the mountainside, he returned to the Australian embassy in Kathmandu to find that his passport had been turned in by his climbing partners with the explanation that he had died on the slopes of Mount Everest.

The man who had been so lovingly nursed back to health was—in his life in Australia—a trained nurse. After having his worldly possessions sent to him from home, he returned to the Sherpas to repay their kindness by living, working, and caring for his new "chosen people."

My brother is a teacher who doubles as the golf coach for an inner-city high school. When his first "team" showed up, he had four excited boys—only one of whom had even played miniature golf—and no equipment. Doing what he could, he scrounged up some old clubs from his and our father's collection and managed to put together three mismatched sets that they could share.

One day he was playing golf with some people he didn't know and mentioned in the course of the conversation his golf team and their unusual equipment. The next Monday morning he was called down to the school office. One of the men he had played golf with had shown up at the school with four complete sets of clubs, with golf bags and wood covers, each equipped with three dozen new balls.

My brother wanted to thank the man but didn't remember his name, so he wrote a letter to the local newspaper and it ran on the front page of the sports section. Within two weeks the school had received so much equipment that they were able to donate several sets of clubs to other inner-city schools for their fledgling golf teams.

When you are kind to someone in trouble, you hope they'll remember and be kind to someone else. And it'll become like a wildfire.

—Whoopi Goldberg

Sympathy: Two hearts tugging at one load.

—Charles H. Parkhurst

Twelve years ago I came home from grocery shopping to a message that my husband had been killed in a freak auto accident. Totally aside from the devastating emotional toll it took on me, I was completely unprepared to cope with the myriad things that needed to be done. Without asking, or for that matter seemingly without any planning whatsoever, my neighbors simply extended their circle of chores to encompass my small farm.

One day my cornfield was harvested; repairs to my roof and barn just appeared. My vegetable garden was always weeded and seemed more productive than ever before—soon vegetables that I didn't remember planting were ripening. I would come home to find a pile of wood, cut and stacked and ready to get me through the winter. Pies, breads, jams, and cases of canned tomatoes appeared at my door and in my pantry.

It all seems so unreal now: whatever was needed simply manifested. When the help was no longer needed, it no longer appeared. It was like some kind of beautiful self-correcting dance of kindness. I will be forever grateful to all those wonderful people.

Live as if **everything** you do will eventually be **known.**

—Hugh Prather

Service is the rent we pay for being.
It is the very purpose of life
and not something you do in your spare time.

—Marian Wright Edelman

Each small task of everyday life
is part of the total harmony of the universe.

—*St. Thérèse of Lisieux*

WHILE RIDING THE BUS to work one day, I noticed a small boy—no more than six or seven—board the bus. I was surprised that no adult accompanied him. With an oversized backpack on his back, it was obvious he was on his way to school, and he asked the driver to call out his stop. He sat so adult-like in the front of the bus. I watched his small legs dangling off the seat, unable to reach the floor. The bus driver called out his stop and waited patiently while the boy attempted to cross the busy street. Cars continued to whiz by. Then the driver put on the emergency brake, stepped off the bus, and took the boy's hand to lead him across the street. My heart filled with emotion. As I was leaving I got the driver's name and wrote a letter to the transit company, thanking them for having such a wonderful employee.

**To do good is to do so
in the minute particular. The general good is
the refuge of the fool and the scoundrel.**

—William Blake

When I was six years old my mother took me to school on opening day. Sometime during that first day, a small boy started to cry. I immediately went over to him and put my arms around him. The teacher ordered me to return to my assigned seat. I could not believe the teacher's indifference toward this boy because whenever I cried at home, some member of my family would be right there with their arms around me.

My teacher kept telling me to leave the boy alone, and I kept refusing to obey her until the boy stopped crying. I went home that day with a note to my mother stating that I was rude, disobedient, and a troublemaker. I explained to my mother just what had happened, and she came back to school with me the next day. She told my teacher that I had been taught to be considerate and caring toward others and that I was not likely to change. She strongly advised my teacher to get used to my sympathetic nature.

That incident happened seventy-two years ago, and I have enjoyed hugging a lot of troubled people since then.

T'was her thinking of others
that made you think of her.

—Elizabeth Browning

If you think you are too small to be effective, you have never been in bed with a mosquito.

—BETTY REESE

If I can stop one heart from breaking,
I shall not live in vain:
If I can ease one life the aching,
Or cool one pain,
Or help one fainting robin
Unto his nest again,
I shall not live in vain.

—*Emily Dickinson*

A FEW YEARS AGO I had managed to screw up my life so badly that I found myself without a home and without hope. I'm ashamed to admit it, but even then I was so absorbed by my own self-pity that all I could think of was begging enough money to buy the cheapest drink I could find. One day I was sitting in front of a store panhandling when a woman walked by with a small boy in tow. She ignored my pitch and hurried away. As I watched them go down the sidewalk, the small boy broke free and came running back. He stood in front of me, fumbling in his coat pocket; he pulled out a five-dollar bill—what was almost certainly more money then he had ever held before—and handed it to me.

I was completely dumbstruck and just sat there staring at him with the money in my hand. By then his mother had returned, and with tears in her eyes gently led the boy away. He turned back once to wave and then they were gone. I don't know how long I sat there, but I have not had another drink since then.

Engrave this upon my heart:
**There isn't anyone you couldn't love
once you've heard their story.**

—MARY LOU KOWNACKI

Do not wait for leaders;

do it alone,

person to person.

—MOTHER TERESA

The key word for our time is practice.
We have all the **light** we need,
we just have to put it into practice.

—PEACE PILGRIM

To share often and much . . .
to know even one life has breathed easier
because you have lived.
This is to have succeeded.

—RALPH WALDO EMERSON

ONE NIGHT around midnight in my third year of high school I was driving through a very rich neighborhood when I spotted a small boy walking along the road. He seemed so out of place that I pulled over to see if he needed any help. When I opened my door I could see that he was about eight years old and was crying. I asked him where he was going and if he needed a ride home, but he wouldn't answer me. Finally I just said, "Here, get in the car and we'll go get some ice cream or something." He quite willingly got in, but then wouldn't answer anything more than yes or no.

Before starting the car, I got a twenty-dollar bill out of my purse and told him to hold it until we found an ice cream store. Then as we were searching, I kept asking where he lived and offering to take him home. Finally he said, "No, please, they're mean to me. I ran away."

 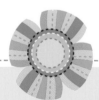

I asked him if he lived with both his parents, and he told me that he lived with his father and stepmother. He said he wanted to be with his mother, but she lived in Texas.

We drove around for about an hour, never finding an open ice cream store, and he still refused to be taken home. Finally he told me where his best friend lived, so I took him there and gave him my phone number. On the way back to the car I remembered the twenty-dollar bill I had given him and assumed he still had it. When I got in the car the money was lying on the passenger seat. I remember smiling, hoping he would be okay and thinking that he had probably just had a fight with his father.

A week later I got a call from his friend's parents, telling me that they had found iron burns across his back and other cuts and bruises. He ended up being sent to his mother in Texas after a big court battle. It made me feel so blessed to have been able to play a part in helping him escape from the brutal world he had been living in.

A FEW YEARS AGO my three-year-old son had a nasty fall and ended up at the local hospital. It turned out that the fall was the least of our worries. The doctors found a tumor the size of a softball in his left lung. We were all scared to death, and the doctors were not too optimistic. Throughout this traumatic development a male nurse showed great compassion toward my son.

Surgery was ordered immediately for the next day, and my son had to go through a tough procedure to get ready. To my distress the wonderful nurse was just about to sign off for the day, and the nurse replacing him was one who hated her job; I casually mentioned to the man that I wished he was going to be on duty instead.

A little while later he reappeared and stayed with us, helping out even though he was off duty. He even arranged to change his shift the next day so that when my son came out of surgery he would be there to soothe his fears. I will never forget what he did, and today when I look at my son, who is better than anyone thought possible, I truly believe that the sincere caring of this nurse was instrumental in his being able to keep trying.

The center of human nature
is rooted in
ten thousand ordinary acts of kindness
that define our days.

—*Stephen Jay Gould*

Always, Sir,
set a high value
on spontaneous kindness.

—Samuel Johnson

Once when I was sixteen and learning to drive, I motioned to a driver to go ahead of me, and he didn't acknowledge what I had done. Self-righteously I said, "I'll never do that again!" My father asked me to pull over and said, "You're not kind to people because they'll thank you. You're kind to people because it's the right thing to do. You're kind to people because it helps the other person and because it helps you." That was fifteen years ago and I've tried to live my life from that perspective ever since. I can still hear my father's gentle voice asking me, "Your attitude, action, comment—will it add to the sadness and hurt of the world? Or will it add to the love and the kindness which might heal us and make us whole? It's your choice."

Give what you have.
To someone, it may be better
than you dare to think.

—*Henry Wadsworth Longfellow*

One can never pay in gratitude;
one can only pay "in kind" somewhere else in life.

—Anne Morrow Lindbergh

When I was young, I admired clever people.
Now that I am old, I admire kind people.

—Abraham Heschel

SAY LITTLE and **DO MUCH.**

—*Shammai*

My marriage had come apart in a dramatic and violent fashion that left me shaking and scared to death. I escaped with two small children, a broken-down car, and $423 in cash. I was so scared that I drove aimlessly for hundreds of miles, determined to get so completely lost that we could not be found. Not a single person knew where we had gone. After sleeping in the car for a couple of days, I found a run-down old house outside a small town and put down almost the last of my money for rent. I was scared and broke but at least we had a place to start over. I spent the next day looking for work and came "home" to our sad and empty nest on the verge of tears, not at all sure we would make it.

There, sitting on the sagging front porch, were five bags of groceries, a large box of pots, pans, and kitchen utensils, and a vase of the most beautiful irises I had ever seen. I must have cried for ten minutes before I could pull myself together to unpack our miraculous gifts. No note, no explanation. I could not imagine who had done it, who could possibly have known how desperate we were. That was many years ago, and sitting on top of my stove in my beautiful modern kitchen is an old, battered whistle-blowing teapot, reminding me when I boil water for my morning coffee of the beautiful gift of kindness that was given to me in my hour of greatest need.

Two years ago a sixty-eight-year-old woman was the victim of a burglary. She lived simply on a fixed income, and the only item of value—her television—was stolen. After saving for nearly a year she bought a new one. Then, returning home one afternoon from a visit with her sister, she found a police officer waiting for her. Her home had been burglarized again, and again her television had been taken; this left her scared, shaken, and without access to what was a regular part of her day.

This time the story turned out differently. After hearing her plight, the officer in charge of the investigation negotiated a deal with a local electronics store that resulted in a brand-new television arriving in time for her sixty-ninth birthday.

What do we live for, if it is not to make life less difficult for each other?

—GEORGE ELIOT

Be kind—everyone you meet is fighting a hard battle.

—John Watson

I AM A SENIOR IN HIGH SCHOOL and work at a shoe store. One day a woman and her six-year-old son came in to buy school shoes. They found a pair he liked and came to the register to pay for them. As the woman was unfolding her checkbook, I noticed that she had temporary checks and had to tell her that store policy would not let me accept her check.

Her son had been prancing around the store, testing out his new shoes and showing them to everyone; when she told him he had to take them off, tears started to well up in his eyes. It just broke my heart. I stopped him before he could untie them, pulled out my checkbook, and wrote a check for the shoes. His mother could not believe what I was doing. She wrote a temporary check out to me and gave me her address and telephone number so I would know that I could trust her.

As she walked out of the store she told me she would never forget me. It was not until later that I noticed she had made out the check for ten dollars more than the shoes cost. And at the bottom of the check on the memo line she had written: "For the nice woman at the shoe store."

$\mathcal{W}$e make a living by what we get,
but we make a life by what we give.

–Norman MacEwan

I drive a taxicab in San Diego and have seen thousands of acts of kindness. One of the most wonderful came when the stepfather of our dispatcher died, and the dispatcher could not afford the ticket to fly back to New Jersey for the funeral. All day long pledges of money kept coming in over the radio. It was just like a private telethon. Cab drivers and even passengers who heard what was happening over the radio started emptying their pockets. We raised the plane fare in no time.

The end result of wisdom is . . . **good deeds.**

—Babylonian Talmud

LAST YEAR I had occasion to get acquainted with a homeless man who lived at the top of a freeway off-ramp in Los Angeles. Every day on my way to work as I sat waiting for the light to change I would talk to Ed about life, homelessness, hopefulness, and the weather—the weather being of vital importance to Ed. We became close, always asking about the other's family—mine in L.A., his on the East Coast. He rarely asked me for money, and I usually tried to bring him some food. Once when he had dental problems I brought him bananas, dried soup, and aspirin. Ed had many other "regulars" who tried to help out.

When I decided to leave L.A. for a job in Florida, I had one final detail to attend to—my car. It was an ugly 1972 Dodge Dart, but it ran great. I had put a lot of money into it but the most I could get for it was $90 from a wrecking yard. I wanted it to go to someone who could and would make use of it, and Ed was the logical choice, He had dreams and plans; he wanted to return to trade school, which he'd had to drop out of as a younger man.

The week before I left, I offered to give Ed the car. With enthusiasm he accepted, going on and on about it being the answer to his problems. We took care of the paperwork, I paid for his license renewal, and then delivered the car with cans of oil, air and oil filters, and a trunk (he calls it his garage) full of paper plates, paper towels, canned food, clothes and—an L.A. essential—an earthquake kit.

As we stood next to the car on a Saturday morning, Ed said he had worked out a deal with a local parking lot owner: he would sweep the lot every day in exchange for a covered place to park his "house." He told me that he had been offered a job as a dishwasher in a new upscale restaurant near his off-ramp. It turns out that another driver who regularly gave Ed money and food had bought the restaurant and asked him to work there at a really good wage. As we hugged good-bye, I said, "Ed, it looks like your ship has come in." He replied with tears in his eyes, "Hell, it's not only come in, I get to go on board."

You have not lived a perfect day, even though you have earned your money, unless you have done something for someone who will never be able to repay you.

—Ruth Smeltzer

The Sufis advise us to speak only after
our words have managed to pass through three gates.
As the first gate, we ask ourselves,

"Are these words true?"

If so, we let them pass on; if not, back they go.
As the second gate, we ask,

"Are they necessary?"

At the last gate, we ask, **"Are they kind?"**

—Eknath Easwaran

It's no use trying to be clever—
we are all clever here; just try to be kind—
a little kind.

—DR. F.J. FOAKES JACKSON

**The fragrance of the rose
lingers on the hand of the giver.**

—Anonymous

I had just moved out of a recovery house after spending six months battling an addiction to alcohol and drugs. I was standing at a bus stop looking through the classifieds, hoping to find a job I was capable of doing. Without a high school education and with my work experience limited to waitressing, the options seemed depressingly limited. At that point my self esteem was stuck to the bottom of my shoes and it diminished with each ad I read.

I looked up from the paper to see an elderly man sitting in his car. He asked me if I wanted a ride and I accepted—knowing what a foolish thing I was doing and even secretly hoping that he would put an end to it all for me. He asked me where I was going and what I was doing. I said I did not know. Then he simply asked me, "If you could do anything you wanted to do, what would it be?"

I blurted out that I would go back to school. I immediately felt stupid for saying it because I doubted I ever could. A few minutes later he pulled into the parking lot of the local community college, pointed out the admissions office, and told me I would find what I needed in there. Trembling and insecure, I filled out the registration papers.

As I write this, I have received my associate of arts degree and am planning to study toward a BA in journalism and an MA in psychology. My life has turned around 180 degrees, and I owe a lot of that to a man whose name I don't even know.

Enrique slipped across the Mexican border three years ago with a dream common in this country: to work hard and make a better life for himself. He worked the fields of California and lived in the shadows of society until he showed up at a county hospital one day with a large tumor on the back of his head. Diagnosed with a treatable case of lymphoma, Enrique came up against a harsh reality: his cancer was completely curable, but without treatment he would be dead within six months—and the state's "safety net" for medical treatment no longer pays to care for illegal immigrants.

Indeed, the hospital routinely turns away those too poor to pay, but Enrique's life-and-death plight caused many of the healthcare professionals involved to pause and reconsider. Meetings were held, ethics debated. As his treating physician said: "Ethically, the situation is not at all unclear—this is a matter of life or death. If Enrique were a wealthier person or born in a different place, he'd be getting treatment. The system has gotten so crazy that we can look at a young, healthy guy and say, 'Sorry.'"

But instead of saying sorry, a small group of health workers decided to do something about it. Doctors at the hospital donated their time to treat Enrique, but the treatment itself—radiation, expensive drugs, and hospital stays—also cost a lot. So they approached a number of pharmaceutical companies and two offered to donate medication. Then they went public and donations began flowing in for the rest of the expenses.

Enrique will get his chance at life because enough people cared.

It's amazing how much people can get done if they don't worry about who gets the credit.

—SANDRA SWINNEY

When we come to the edge
Of all the light we have
And we must take a step into
The darkness of the unknown,
We must believe one of two things:
Either we will find something
Firm to stand on
Or we will be taught to fly.

—Anonymous, from "I Can Cope,"
a support organization for people living with cancer

Independence? That's middle-class blasphemy. We are all dependent on one another, every soul of us on earth.

—George Bernard Shaw

I WAS QUIETLY WORKING ONE DAY when I heard a very distressed voice coming from a nearby office. The walls were thin and I could not help but hear the conversation taking place. A woman I did not know had been counting on borrowing money from a colleague, but circumstances made it impossible for him to help her. I have no idea what possessed me, but without even asking what she needed it for I found myself going to the bank and withdrawing $1,000 to lend to a woman I did not even know.

Several months later after a series of life's ever-surprising turns, I found myself jobless, homeless, and, I thought, friendless. I also needed medical care in order to even begin looking for a new job. The woman to whom I had lent the money was not in a position to return it, but she ended up repaying me anyway—and then some. First, she used her medical training

to help me physically get back on my feet. Then she had her son, who owned a small moving business, come collect my belongings—and arranged for her boyfriend to stay with her while I stayed in his apartment. I now had the three things a homeless person needs most: an address, a telephone, and a shower. As a bonus, the apartment came with a lovely cat that went with the territory and gave me great comfort in that difficult time.

It wasn't too long before I was able to find work and move to a home of my own. That was thirteen years ago, and since then the woman and I have become life-long friends and business partners. To her it was a miracle that anyone could give so much money to a stranger; to me it was a miracle that anyone could come up with such a basketful of solutions custom-made to fit my needs.

**Since you get more joy out of
giving joy to others,
you should put a good deal of thought
into the happiness that you are able to give.**

—Eleanor Roosevelt

There is an older woman in our town who is simply incredible. She has lived a very difficult life, full of suffering. Two of her children died, one from a terrible lingering disease and the other in an automobile accident. Her husband had a very bad stroke many years ago and then lingered on for twenty years before dying. Yet she is the most generous and compassionate person I have ever met.

One day, I asked her how she could still wake up every day with a smile and a kind word for everyone around her. She looked at me with this really surprised expression on her face and said, "Oh, but my life has been full of so many wonderful people. We all have our troubles, but those are only doorways we must walk through. Each of the terrible things that happened to me also brought me some unexpected surprises—moments of connection with others, opportunities to become a better person. I guess I do wish it could have been easier, but really I feel that my life has been blessed nonetheless."

My brother-in-law used to be the black hole of the family. He sucked up everybody's energy, complained like mad, and never gave anything back. We were always rescuing him from various scrapes and receiving precious little thanks. Then, when he was thirty-seven, he was hospitalized with a very rare brain tumor. For a couple of months, it was touch-and-go as to whether he would survive at all and, if so, how much brain damage he would sustain. Fortunately, he made out just fine, and the amazing thing is that when he got out of the hospital he was a completely changed man. Now he's the one who brightens up every family occasion with his humor and

positiveness—the one all the kids gravitate to. He has become more responsible toward his family and is consistently grateful for anything you might do for him. The difference is like night and day.

It doesn't matter how long we may have been stuck in a sense of our limitations. If we go into a darkened room and turn on the light, it doesn't matter if the room has been dark for a day, or a week, or ten thousand years—we turn on the light and it is illuminated. Once we contact our capacity for love and happiness . . . the light has been turned on.

—*Sharon Salzberg*

I HAVE BEEN GOING to the same bagel/coffee shop every Sunday for years. One morning in the middle of a dreary and drizzly weekend, I trudged in dripping wet with my newspaper carefully tucked under my overcoat and ordered my usual bagel with lox and cream cheese and an espresso. I was casually informed that my coffee had already been paid for. I looked around expecting to see some friend sitting somewhere but didn't, and when I asked, the young woman at the register just smiled and said someone paid for twenty coffees and you are number eight. I sat there for almost an hour, reading my paper, and watching more surprised people come in to find their morning coffee pre-paid. There we all were, furtively at first and then with big funny smiles on our faces, looking at everyone else in the restaurant trying to figure out who had done this incredible thing, but mostly just enjoying the experience as a group. It was a beautiful blast of sunshine on an otherwise overcast winter day.

Our brightest blazes of gladness
are commonly kindled by unexpected sparks.

—Samuel Johnson

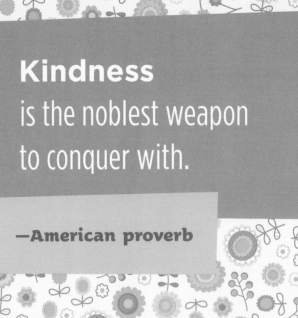

Kindness
is the noblest weapon
to conquer with.

—American proverb

I feel so lucky and so blessed. After fifty years of marriage, I look around me and see so few relationships that last with any fun, fire, or passion. So many times, people have asked us what our secret is, and I am always at a loss about how to respond. It has always been easy. I have heard my husband insist that he could never do enough to repay me for my kindness and understanding to him, and it always amazes me, because I am just as convinced that it is I who can never do enough to repay him. If I had to explain the success of our relationship very simply, I guess I would have to say that we are very kind to each other, every day, and in every way possible.

Love means to love that which is unlovable;
or it is no virtue at all.

—G.K. Chesterton

- -

Many years ago, there was an old man in our town who used to irritate everyone. He walked around with a Bible under his arm, always ready to shout scripture. One of his favorite targets was homosexuals. He'd stand outside the local gay coffee shop, castigating everyone who went in or out.

At some point, it became obvious that he was really sick, and it turned out that he had gotten HIV from a blood transfusion. At that time, the only people who were really doing outreach and support for HIV/AIDS patients were in the gay community. Even though they knew him well from the years of abuse, they took him under their wing. At first, he was incredibly ungrateful and abusive, but as his body weakened, he lost some of his old anger. He spent the last months of his life in a hospice surrounded by gay men. They were his only support and his only comfort, and when he died, they were his only friends.

ONE SUMMER when my brother and I were still in high school, we were laying on the front lawn, bored silly, and he said, "You know, old lady Henderson sure has let her yard go." Right there, we hatched a plan to make a midnight gardening raid. The next day, Mrs. Henderson was standing out in her yard, talking about how some elves had transformed her overgrown garden into neatly trimmed bushes. It was so much fun that we planned a raid on another neighbor's yard a few days later. When the sun rose the day after, the hedge around the yard across the street was all trimmed. My mother must have figured out it was us, because later that day she made some comment about how the corner lot sure would look better with some flowers along the sidewalk instead of that bare patch of dirt, and later that afternoon we discovered four flats of flowers sitting in our garage just waiting for the midnight raiders.

It was great fun, and we lasted almost a month before we finally got caught—there is just no way to mow a lawn silently. It not only brought smiles to the entire neighborhood, but people started taking better care of their yards, and we even ended up getting some gardening jobs.

All my life I have tried to

pluck a thistle and plant a flower
wherever the flower would grow
in thought and mind.

—Abraham Lincoln, inspired by his beloved mother's credo,
which was **kindness to neighbors and strangers**

No one is rich enough to do without a neighbor.

—Danish proverb

By the accident of fortune
a man may rule the world for a time,
**but by virtue of love and kindness
he may rule the world forever.**

—LAO-TSU

He that is kind is free, though he is a slave;
he that is evil is a slave, though he be a king.

—*St. Augustine*

In the words of one great prayer:

"Bless me into usefulness."

—Sogyal Rinpoche

A story I want to tell was passed down in my family from my great-grandfather. He was a young captain from Pennsylvania fighting in the Civil War. In preparation for a coming battle, he had requisitioned a beautiful Georgia plantation home as a field hospital. He told the lady of the house to leave before the battle started, but she responded, "I am staying. There will be wounded and I can be useful." For four days, her land was occupied and turned into a bloody battlefield while she tirelessly did everything she could to ease the suffering of the wounded and dying Union soldiers. Word of her care spread through the troops, and when they were leaving, every man turned and saluted as they passed her home.

My great-grandfather said that it was the most enduring memory he had of that horrible war, because it reminded him that even in the midst of an incredibly brutal and savage experience, one person's simple kindness could still shine through.

GENTLENESS is everywhere in daily life, a sign that faith rules through ordinary things: through cooking and small talk, through storytelling, making love, fishing, tending animals and sweet corn and flowers, through sports, music, and books, raising kids—all the places where the gravy soaks in and grace shines through. Even in a time of elephantine vanity and greed, one never has to look far to see the campfires of gentle people.

–Garrison Keillor

A man's true wealth is the good he does in the world.

—MOHAMMED

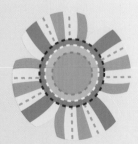